THE 4-DAY BATTLE OF MIDWAY

HISTORY BOOK FOR 12 YEAR OLD CHILDREN'S HISTORY

BABY PROFESSOR
EDUCATION KIDS

Speedy Publishing LLC

40 E. Main St. #1156

Newark, DE 19711

www.speedypublishing.com

Copyright 2017

World War II raged around the world from 1939 to 1945. In the war in the Pacific, one of the key battles was for control of Midway Island. Learn how the fate of the war hinged on four days of fighting.

THE JAPANESE PLAN

In World War II two countries, Germany and Japan, were each trying to become the dominant country in their part of the world. They were allies as part of the "Axis powers".

WORLD WAR II

COAST OF JAPAN 1945

Japan wanted to become a great power on equal footing with the British Empire and with the United States. It had seen how a powerful country like China could become overwhelmed by countries with better technology and better armies, and it did not want the same fate for itself.

To become and stay powerful in the world, a country needs (among other things) resources from which to make things from weapons to fuel, from vehicles and their tires to consumer goods. Japan is short on many raw materials. It did not want to rely on trade to get what it needed, so the only other choice was conquest.

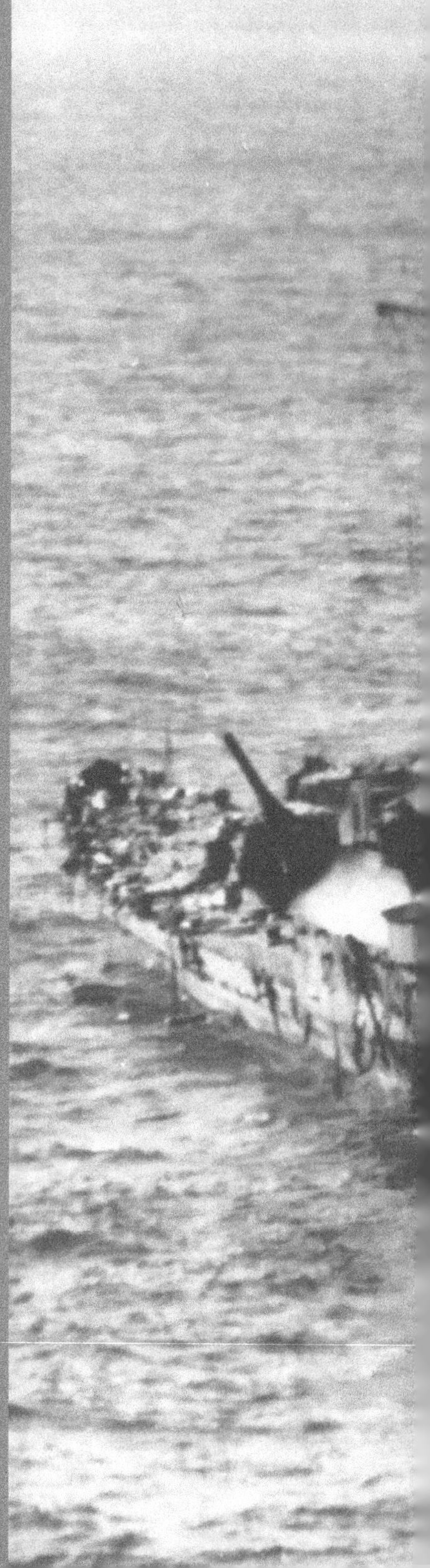

JAPANESE CRUISER

BATTLE OF MANILA

In the 1930s one plan was for Japan to attack the Soviet Union with a goal of gaining a lot of territory with forests and mines, but not much population. However, Japan lost a badly-managed war with the Soviet Union in Manchuria in 1938. Japanese leadership decided they would have better success conquering the Pacific islands like the Philippines and Borneo, and the countries of Southeast Asia, while continuing an attempt to gain control of China.

Japan knew it would have to fight Great Britain, with its powerful bases in Hong Kong and Singapore, as well as current and former parts of the British Empire like India and Australia. It did not want to also have to fight the United States at the same time. If it could knock the United States out of the war early, that would make it easier for Japan to defeat its remaining opponents.

WORLD WAR II

ATTACK ON PEARL HARBOR

When Japan launched a sneak attack against the U.S. naval base at Pearl Harbor in Hawaii, in December, 1941, the goal was to destroy the American navy in the Pacific Ocean. The attack was devastating, but it did not completely succeed.

The Japanese leadership decided the next step should be an attack on Midway Island, over one thousand miles northwest of Hawaii, in June of 1942. There were two goals: one was capturing the island and destroying U.S. forces there. The second goal was to lure the remaining U.S. ships into the area in an attempt to defend the island so planes from Japanese aircraft carriers, plus attacks from submarines, could destroy them. If the U.S. lost its fleet and saw Japan in place in Midway readying an attack on Hawaii, perhaps that would drive the Americans out of the war.

BATTLE OF MIDWAY

BEFORE THE BATTLE

Japan scheduled its main assault against Midway on June 4, followed by an invasion June 6. The Combined Fleet that sailed east in May, 1942 had powerful attack ships, especially aircraft carriers, and troop ships carrying the invasion forces. The four aircraft carriers taking part were among the most powerful ships in the Pacific Ocean.

JAPANESE BATTLESHIP

The fleet moved in several units spread far apart from each other. Admiral Yamamoto's plan was to conceal the size of the attacking forces until the last moment, when they would converge on Midway. He hoped the U.S. planes would spot only one of the groups, and that American ships would respond without being prepared for how powerful the enemy force was.

STRONG AND WEAK INTELLIGENCE

A major flaw in these plans was that the American forces had cracked the secret Japanese code, and U.S. high command knew how many ships were coming, where they would rendezvous, and what their plans were. In addition, aerial patrols spotted various parts of the enemy fleet quite early, and were able to report back on its progress.

Admiral Chester Nimitz and the rest of U.S. high command scrambled to assemble enough forces to meet an attack from four or five aircraft carriers. They even pressed into service the USS Yorktown, an aircraft carrier that had already been damaged so badly in an earlier battle the Japanese had written it off as sunk. Yorktown was rushed through repairs so it could join two other carriers, Enterprise and Hornet, in defending Midway.

USS YORKTOWN

At another level the U.S. had intelligence that was superior to Japan's. For many years the U.S. had been working on "fleet problem" exercises involving two forces with aircraft carriers attacking each other. The U.S. concluded that the force that first located the enemy and was able to launch its planes in an attack was almost always the force that won.

The U.S. developed long-range carrier-capable planes that could both scout and deliver heavy bombs, as first-strike weapons.

X-152
243925
X-151
243925
151

By contrast, Japanese planning was based on the experiences of Japan's war in China. Attacking and destroying enemy airfields and supply bases required massed attacks of waves of bombers, not individual bombers. The Japanese used float planes launched from cruisers and battleships to do their scouting, and held back their carrier-based planes to be ready for mass attacks.

FOUR DAYS OF FIGHTING

On June 3, the first U.S. planes attacked the Japanese carriers. The first attacks were not successful and most of the planes were shot down.

JAPANESE AIRCRAFT CARRIER

BATTLE OF MIDWAY

On June 4, the four Japanese carriers launched most of their planes in a mass attack on Midway. Planes from Midway tried to hit the carriers, but were not successful. The attack on Midway caused heavy damage, but did not disable the base as the Japanese had hoped.

NATC
308
NATC 308

Torpedo bombers from U.S. carriers launched an attack against the Japanese forces but did not succeed.

Then luck favored the U.S. forces. At the same time that the Japanese planes returned from the Midway attack, needing to land and refuel on the carriers, three squadrons of U.S. dive bombers began their attack. The Japanese carriers had little or no air cover, and the bombers were able to hit and sink

three of the four carriers. The last carrier, the Hiryu, continued to fight long enough to launch an attack that damaged the Yorktown. Planes from the Yorktown and the Enterprise then sank the Hiryu.

Having lost almost all of its airborne force, and with no way to protect troops as they invaded Midway Island, the Japanese abandoned the attack and headed for home waters. The battle continued into June 6, when U.S. planes sank a Japanese cruiser and a Japanese submarine torpedoed the already-damaged Yorktown and sank it.

USS YORKTOWN

ATTACK ON PEARL HARBOR

MIDWAY FACTS

The Japanese lost all four of the large aircraft carriers it had sent to the attack on Midway. This left Japan with just two large carriers. All four carriers had taken part in the attack on Pearl Harbor.

Along with the four aircraft carriers, Japan lost a heavy cruiser and about 250 aircraft. Over three thousand Japanese sailors and airmen died in the battle. The U.S. lost one aircraft carrier, one destroyer, and about 150 planes. Just over 300 Americans died in the action.

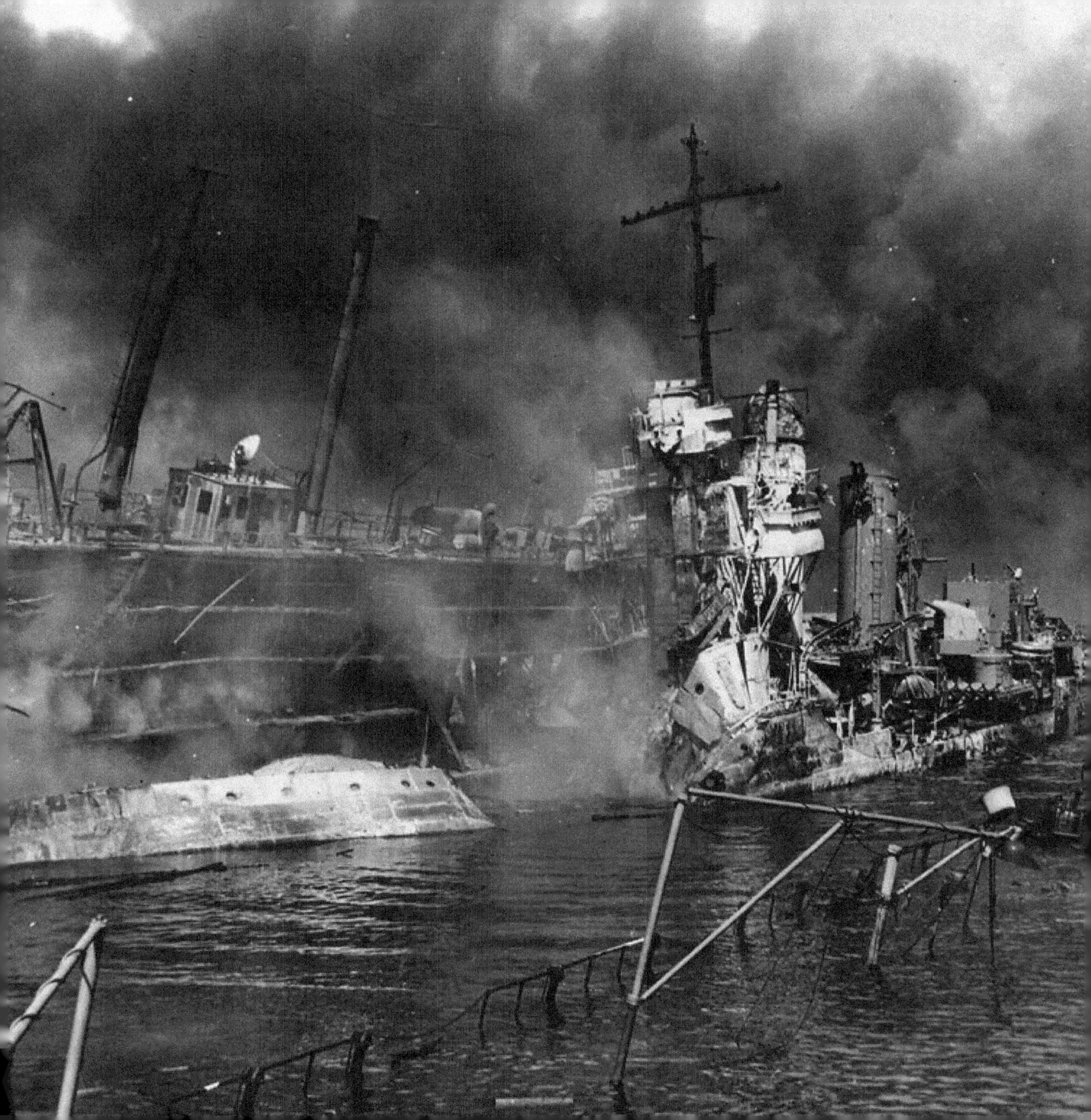

JAPANESE PRISONERS OF WAR

For Japan, the worst loss of the battle was not the ships or the planes, or even the pilots: it was the hundreds of skilled mechanics and air crew members who were essential for repairing and refueling the planes and keeping them flying.

For some reason Japan had reduced production of their best carrier-capable attack aircraft. This meant that the planes used in the battle were mostly inferior in speed and firepower to the U.S. planes they were fighting.

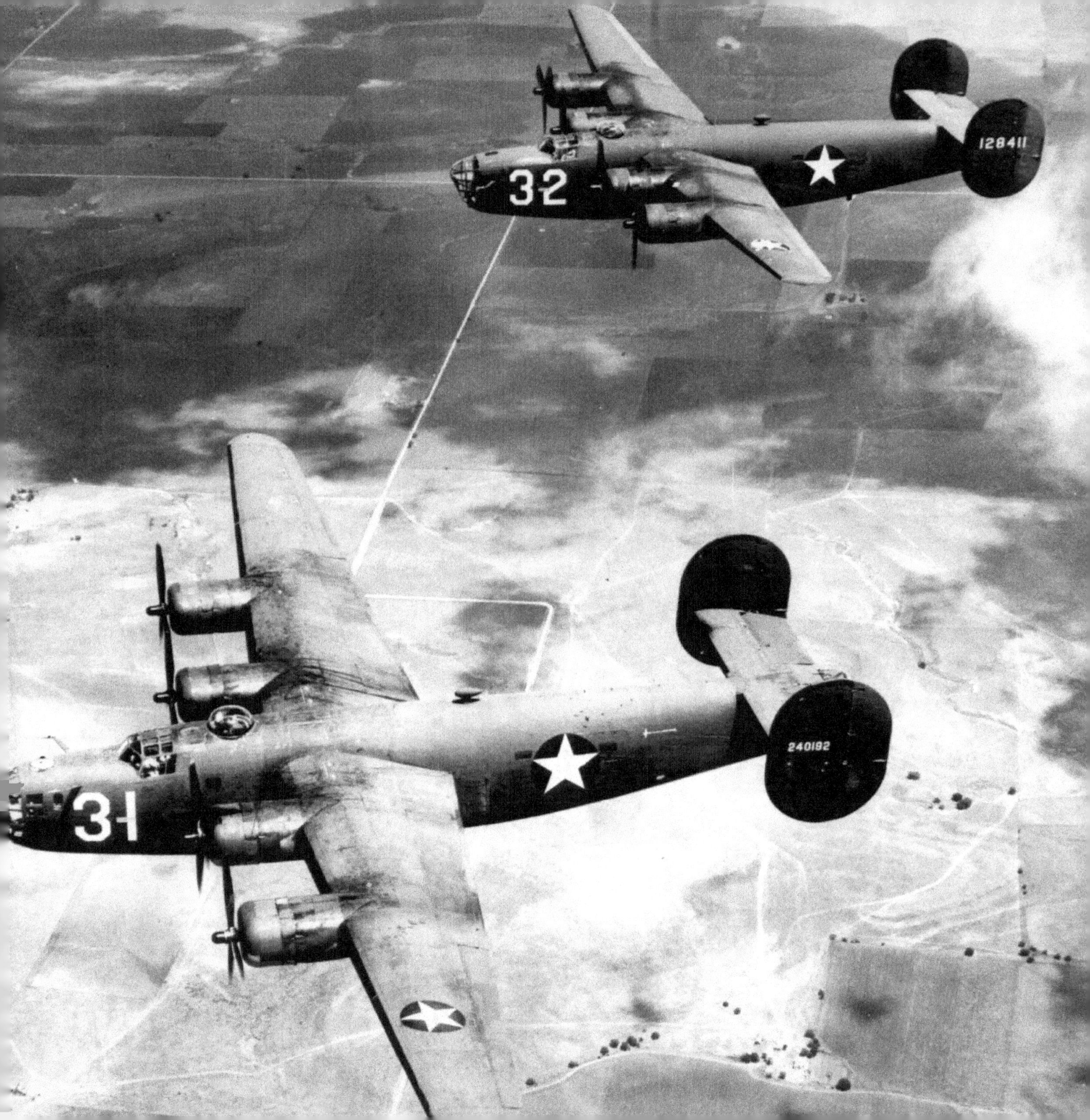

As a diversion from the Midway attack, Japan had also attacked some small islands in the Aleutian Islands chain off Alaska. They captured the islands in the hope that U.S. forces would be diverted from Midway to deal with this attack. This plan did not work, and U.S. forces were able to liberate the islands by May of 1943. The fight for the islands was the only campaign in World War II to take place on United States soil.

THE IMPACT OF MIDWAY

The defeat at Midway was a shock to the Japanese high command, which thought they had developed an unbeatable plan. Historians have called the battle the most decisive engagement in the history of naval warfare.

PEARL HARBOR

Japan immediately set aside any plans for a further attack on Hawaii or a continued attack on Midway. With the Japanese losses, Japanese and U.S. naval forces were more evenly matched than they had been since the attack on Pearl Harbor.

Midway was the first major victory for the United States in the war with Japan. The U.S. was now in position to launch a campaign of liberating the many Pacific islands that Japan had captured and fortified as bases. The first major step in that campaign, the attack on Guadalcanal, began in August, 1942, just two months after Midway.

GUADALCANAL

WORLD WAR II

BATTLE OF MIDWAY
VALUABLE LESSONS LEARNED

The past teaches us so many lessons and lots of interesting facts.

The Battle of Midway teaches us valuable lessons on proper planning, coordination, teamwork, discipline and trust. We must trust our own intelligence and delegate tasks.

Let us learn from what the past has taught us and apply them in our present.

L earn more about the countries and people involved in World War II, why they fought, and what happened, in Baby Professor books like The Axis Powers vs. the Allied Powers in World War II, Women in the Armed Forces, and The Theaters of World War II: Europe and the Pacific.

Visit
BABY PROFESSOR
EDUCATION KIDS
www.BabyProfessorBooks.com
to download Free Baby Professor eBooks
and view our catalog of new and exciting
Children's Books